THE WALLPAINT

GARTON-ON-THE-WOLDS

Jill Allibone

PEVSNER MEMORIAL TRUST

1991

Published by the Pevsner Memorial Trust,
c/o The Courtauld Institute of Art,
Somerset House, The Strand, London WC2R 0RN

© Jill Allibone and Pevsner Memorial Trust 1991

All the photographs are copyright of the Royal Commission on the Historical Monuments of England.

To the memory of
Rosalind Hawkes
Hon. Treasurer, Pevsner Memorial Trust
1985-89

This publication has received financial assistance from Humberside Libraries and Arts and East Yorkshire Borough Council.

Printed and bound by
Clifford Ward & Co. (Bridlington) Ltd.,
55 West Street, Bridlington, East Yorkshire, YO15 3DZ

ISBN 0 9518430 0 1

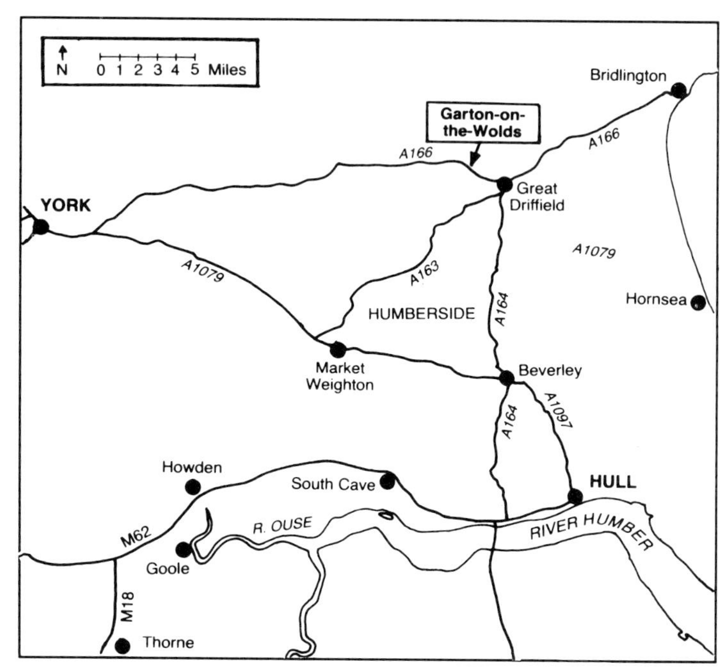

Location of Garton-on-the-Wolds

PREFACE

The Pevsner Memorial Trust was established in 1985 in order to raise money for a major work of conservation in memory of the great architectural historian and critic, Sir Nikolaus Pevsner (1902-83). The Trust chose to conserve the scheme of wallpaintings executed by Clayton and Bell at St. Michael's Church, Garton-on-the-Wolds, for several reasons: first and foremost, it responded to Sir Nikolaus's challenge (written in 1972) in his account of the church in the *York and the East Riding* volume of The Buildings of England, "It is essential that they be preserved", second, his early and consistent advocacy of Victorian architecture made a Victorian project especially suitable, and finally such a complete cycle of Victorian wallpaintings is almost unparalleled in this country, and so on art historical grounds cried out for rescue.

The cost of conservation has exceeded £100,000, and the Trust is grateful for the generous support of hundreds of donors, individuals and trusts, whose contributions in the aggregate amounted to a formidable sum. They cannot be named here individually; but it is right to record by name a number of institutions and charitable trusts, each of which donated £1000 or more: National Heritage Memorial Fund, Department of the Environment, Pilgrim Trust, Esmée Fairbairn Charitable Trust, Pearson plc Charity Trust, Chase Charity, Marc Fitch Fund, Ernest Cook Trust, East Yorkshire Borough Council, F.P. Finn Trust, Goldsmiths' Company, Humberside County Council, Idlewild Trust, Juno Charity Trust, Allen Lane Foundation, Charles James Robertson Trust.

The Trust has been most fortunate in its choice of wallpainting conservators. Donald Smith and Wolfgang Gärtner, with various assistants, have spent a summer season at Garton each year from 1986 to 1991. Their great skill and dedication to their work have ensured that the conservation has been carried out to the highest standards.

Thanks should also be recorded to the Rev. Geoffrey Holman, vicar of Garton, the churchwardens, Mr. Peter Atkinson and Mr. Richard Ullyott, and the parishioners of Garton, who have readily accepted the Trust's intervention, and who have themselves raised and spent under the guidance of their architect Andrew Anderson a large sum of money on repairing the fabric of the church, a work in itself essential to the preservation of the wallpaintings.

The Trust will retain the responsibility for monitoring the condition of the wallpaintings over the coming years, and ensuring in collaboration with the parish that they remain in good condition.

This guidebook has been produced in order to stimulate interest in a remarkable product of Victorian culture. The trust is most grateful to Dr. Jill Allibone for taking time off from her many other commitments in order to research and write it, and to David Neave and Bridget Cherry for seeing it through the press. The illustrations have been made from photographs taken by the Royal Commission on the Historical Monuments of England in the course of a complete photographic record of the conservation work as it progressed. The collaboration of the Commission and the skill of their photographers are greatly appreciated.

John Newman
Chairman
Pevsner Memorial Trust

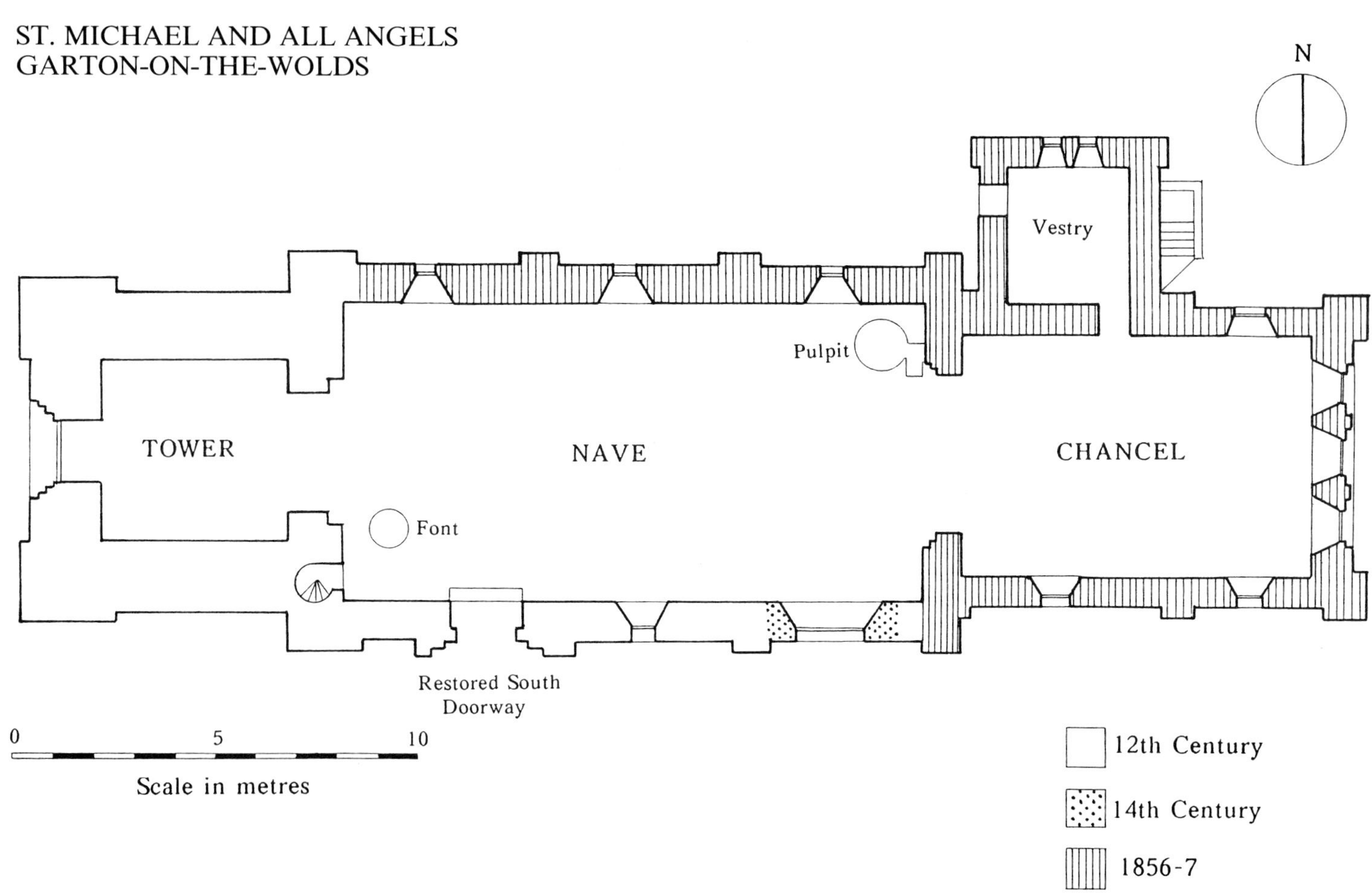

based on a plan provided by Andrew Anderson

INTRODUCTION

The Domesday Book records the presence of a priest and a church at Garton in 1086, and in 1121 it was one of seven churches with which Walter Espec endowed Kirkham Priory, which he founded with his wife Adeline after the death of their only son. Nothing is known about the eleventh century church which would have been a very primitive structure, and this was replaced in the twelfth century by a large but simple building consisting of a nave, a chancel and a west tower.

The lower part of the tower and the south wall of the nave with two round headed windows, are recognisably of this period, as is the west door, which has a round arch with chevron and billet ornament, jamb shafts with scalloped capitals and, above the door, a relief of St. Michael and the dragon flanked by angels. This is now so badly eroded as to be barely legible. A three light window was inserted in the south wall in the 14th century and the top of the tower was rebuilt in the 15th century.

For nearly three hundred years the principal local landowners have been the Sykes family, who first settled in Cumberland, and began to be of substance in the 16th century when a William Sykes became a merchant in Leeds. Two generations later Richard Sykes was a chief Alderman and Magistrate, and his grandson Daniel became Mayor of Hull. His son, Richard, a Baltic merchant, acquired in 1748, by marriage, the Kirkby family's Sledmere estate. He had three sons, Richard, who became High Sheriff in 1752, Mark, who was in holy orders and became a Baronet in 1783, and Joseph who was twice Mayor of Hull. Mark's son Sir Christopher Sykes, the 2nd Baronet, was a Member of Parliament for Beverley and an avid collector of books, and his son, Sir Mark Masterman Sykes, the 3rd Baronet, was the Member for York in 1807-20 and enlarged his father's library at Sledmere. He was also a keen sportsman, bred racehorses and established a pack of foxhounds. When he was succeeded in 1823 by his brother, Sir Tatton, the 4th Baronet, the estate was encumbered with debts.

Sir Christopher had set about improving and enlarging the Sledmere estate by buying up rough grazing cheaply and turning it into arable land during the French wars. He spent thirty years building new farms, planting shelter belts and enclosing moorland, and he acquired the 1,984 acre Garton estate in 1792. Sir Tatton bred sheep and horses, pioneered the use of bone meal as a fertiliser, and as his interests were more sporting than literary, sold his brother's library in order to discharge his inherited debts. He kept the pack of hounds and developed a famous stud, becoming a considerable figure in the hunting, racing and boxing fraternities, but his greatest interest was in the estate, where he built cottages, farms and schools, keeping a close eye on his agent and undertaking manual work, hoeing, hedging and droving, himself. He considered the restoration or rebuilding of parish churches part of the general matter of estate improvement and employed John Loughborough Pearson, a distinguished practitioner of the Gothic Revival, who had built a number of churches in Yorkshire and was later to become the architect of Truro Cathedral, to build a new church at Hilston in 1862, and to restore those at Kirkburn, Bishop Wilton, and Garton-on-the-Wolds.

Pearson first visited Garton in the company of Sykes on the 11th March 1856, the draft contract was ready by the 5th June, and his account for £145.15.0 was rendered on the 19th December 1857. He rebuilt the chancel in the Norman style on the old foundations, incorporating some of the old fabric, with three round-headed east windows with chevron mouldings, and others of a simpler design on the north and south. A vestry was added to the north, and the north wall of the nave and the south door were rebuilt, the latter with a gable, jamb shafts and mouldings, in the manner of the 12th century west door. Pearson's work is distinguished by a most authentic looking corbel table below the eaves, which is characteristic of his correct archaeological approach to restoration work. In the interior he inserted a triple opening in the gable over the chancel arch, an unusual feature that he also uses at Kirkburn. There is no evidence that the church fittings at this date were in any way remarkable. Seats in the chancel, reading and prayer desks and an altar table were all executed by Rattee and Kett in 1857. The total cost was £2,182.16.0.

Sir Tatton died in 1863, and his eldest son, also Sir Tatton, succeeded at the age of 37. He had had a most unhappy childhood, bullied by his father, and grew up to be a strange and lonely man, whose interests were chiefly travel and Gothic architecture. He made immediate changes on the estate, the most significant of which was the dispersal of the famous Sledmere stud in a three day sale. His mother's beloved plants were also done away with, the orangery demolished, the hothouses dismantled and the villagers told to grow cauliflowers, not flowers, in their cottage gardens. He managed the estate efficiently and ruthlessly; incompetent farmers were thrown off their farms, and women who were seen gossiping or children who behaved badly could get their families evicted from their cottages. In 1874, when Sir Tatton was 48, he was tricked into marriage with Christina Anne Jessica Cavendish-Bentinck. Not surprisingly it was to prove a disastrous marriage. However, he was able to gain some relief from an unhappy home life by continuing his father's estate improvements and also his programme of church restoration and embellishment; he began by employing his father's architect.

In 1865 he gave Pearson two commissions, for a village school at Bishop Wilton and some cottages at Sledmere, none of which were built, and also requested him to prepare designs for two new churches at Wansford and Thixendale. These got so far as being advertised for tenders, but at this point Sir Tatton changed his mind, paid Pearson his commission, which came to the considerable sum of £458.17.6., and employed in his place an equally distinguished architect, George Edmund Street, who was later to design the Royal Courts of Justice in the Strand. The reason for this change is not known; it is possible that Sykes may not have liked the designs, but more probably he found Pearson difficult to deal with and slow in getting on with the work. The architect had been devastated by the death of his wife the previous year and this had sadly affected the amount of attention he was giving to his practice. In the end Street took over all Sykes's church work and at Garton he began in 1872 a most remarkable programme of embellishment. Garton was in the gift of the Lord Chancellor, who in 1861 appointed as vicar the Revd. Richard Wrangham, who held the living until 1885, but as Sykes was paying for the works, his views on what should be done no doubt prevailed.

The accounts for both the paintings and the wall tiles in the nave have survived. That from Clayton and Bell, the firm which carried out the murals and the decoration of the roof, is dated July 1876 and shows that the first estimate amounted to £2,500, to which were added extras of £259.4.0. for the dado in the chancel, £297.12.0. for the west wall of the nave, and £12.10.0. for an altar rail, which has now been replaced. The tiles, which are Spanish, were supplied and fixed by F. Garrard of Millwall, London, and cost £166.12.0. Street had made a special study of, and written extensively about Spanish architecture, and this, no doubt, is why such an unusual wall covering for an English parish church is found here. He designed a lych gate in the Romanesque style, which was not built, and also, in 1875, the reredos, which was carved by J. F. Redfern. The chancel screen and the oak font cover, designed by Street in 1875 and 1877 respectively, were both executed by Rattee and Kett of Cambridge.

However, at this point, Sir Tatton dispensed with the services of Street, and returned to Pearson for the completion of the decorative scheme, perhaps because Street had become involved in the work on the Royal Courts of Justice to the extent that it interfered with small commissions in the north of England. In November 1878 Pearson designed new paving for the floors of the chancel and nave, the area within the altar rails was laid with Cosmati work, different coloured marbles set in geometric patterns, and the rest carried out in black, white, yellow and pink mosaic, made by Messrs. George Trollope & Sons of London and installed under the supervision of one of their foremen. New choir stalls executed by Rattee and

Kett were fixed in December 1879 and the following year the painted decoration of the ceiling of the tower was completed by Clayton and Bell, who also made the stained glass windows, which were ready to be sent for installation in the spring of 1879. The font was made in this same year by Trollopes and new lamps were installed in 1881. The nave was reseated in 1899 by Temple Moore, who had by that time become Sir Tatton's preferred architect and had rebuilt the church at Sledmere in 1893.

The wall paintings and stained glass

The most striking of the improvements are beyond doubt the wall paintings and the stained glass. The firm of Clayton and Bell had been founded by John Richard Clayton and Alfred Bell, who had met in the office of the architect George Gilbert Scott; the partnership is chiefly known for their stained glass, but they also worked on a number of schemes which included wall paintings and the general decoration of church interiors. Their first work was a series of windows for the clerestory of the nave of Westminster Abbey in 1856, and in 1859 they were working on stained glass and painted decorations for Scott's All Souls Haley Hill, Halifax. In 1865 they executed the decoration of the chancel of St. Mary the Virgin, Ashley, Northamptonshire after it was rebuilt by Scott. This, apart from purely decorative work, consists of a Christ in Glory above the east window, and along the north and south walls the Apostles and St. Paul, each bearing their attributes, and opposite a series of sixteen Old Testament Prophets, many of whom reappear at Garton. Stylistically the paintings are very similar. Another fine and comprehensive decorative scheme by the firm can be seen at St. Leonard's, Newland, near Great Malvern, begun in 1868 and completed in 1877 and thus contemporary with Garton; this is more complicated than both Ashley and Garton, and consists of biblical scenes, the Seven Acts of Mercy, the Beatitudes, parables, Old Testament figures and saints.

However, the iconography of the wall paintings and stained glass at Garton is unique, in both the breadth of the scheme, and the fact that the images in the murals and the glass relate to each other and jointly illustrate a story or a theme, and are clearly conceived with more than a decorative value in view. In the mid-nineteenth century it was generally believed that the creation myth as told in *Genesis* was a matter of fact, and this view was supported by eminent theologians. In the seventeenth century Archbishop Ussher had, by some unfathomable calculations, fixed the moment of creation as 9am on Sunday, 23rd October 4004 BC, which had been accepted with little argument. So when Charles Darwin published *The Origin of Species by means of Natural Selection* in 1859 his theories were regarded by many as heresy. The orthodox Victorian member of the Church of England believed that the world had been created by God in six days, that man was made in His image, and that all creatures then on earth had survived the biblical flood only because Noah had taken a male and female of each species into the Ark. To deny this struck at the roots of faith and mocked God. But the first edition of Darwin's book sold out on the day of publication, and within a year it had run through three editions. In 1860 Samuel Wilberforce, the Bishop of Oxford, denounced Darwin's theories at the Oxford meeting of the British Association and was successfully confronted by T. H. Huxley. This caused uproar at the time, which did not decrease, and the indignation of the clergy and High Churchmen was exacerbated by Darwin's later publication, *The Descent of Man*, which appeared in 1871. But from the 1860s on there was generally an increasing disbelief in the story of the creation as told in the Bible, which the clergy did their best to combat.

The subjects shown in the paintings suggest that Sir Tatton, possibly at the instigation of the vicar, as no such thing is attempted in any of the other Sykes estate churches, may have taken the proposal to decorate Garton church as an opportunity to ensure that worshippers in this parish were not seduced by scientific theories which flew in the face of divine revelation. The scheme illustrates Old Testament stories in the nave, and scenes from the New Testament in the chancel. The Prophets are shown in the nave, the Apostles and Evangelists in the Chancel. The

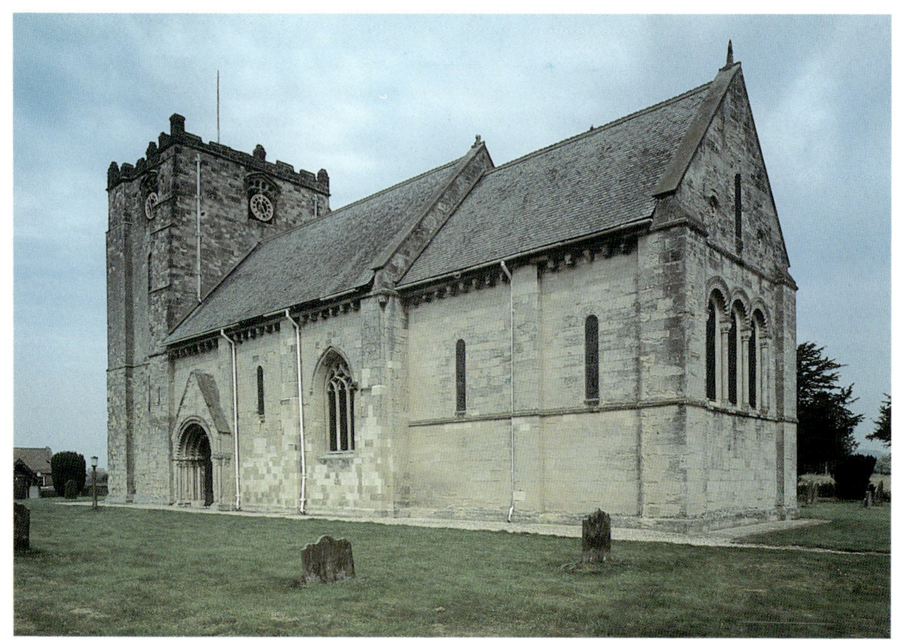

The church of St. Michael, Garton-on-the-Wolds, from the south-east.

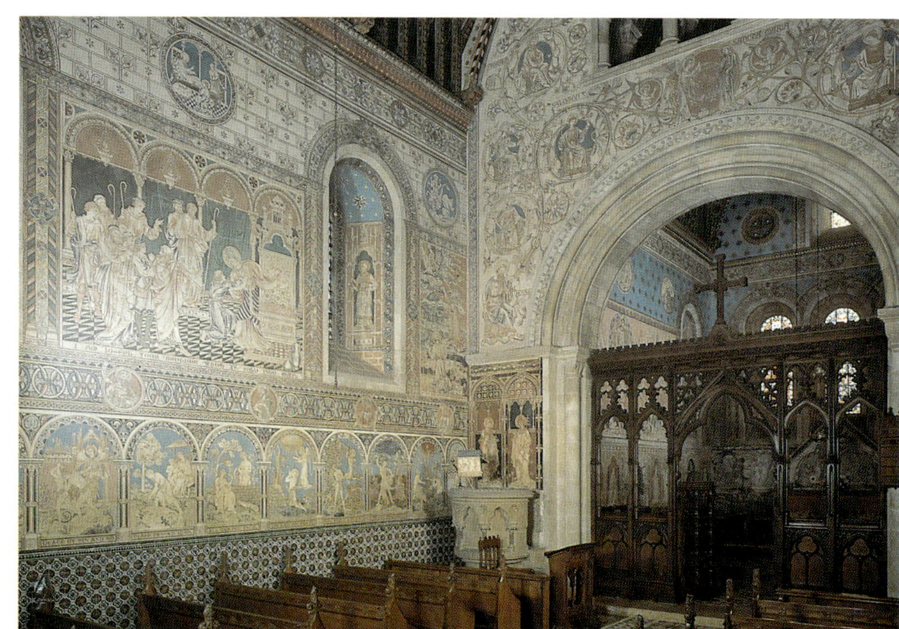

Interior of the church looking from the nave north-east into the chancel.

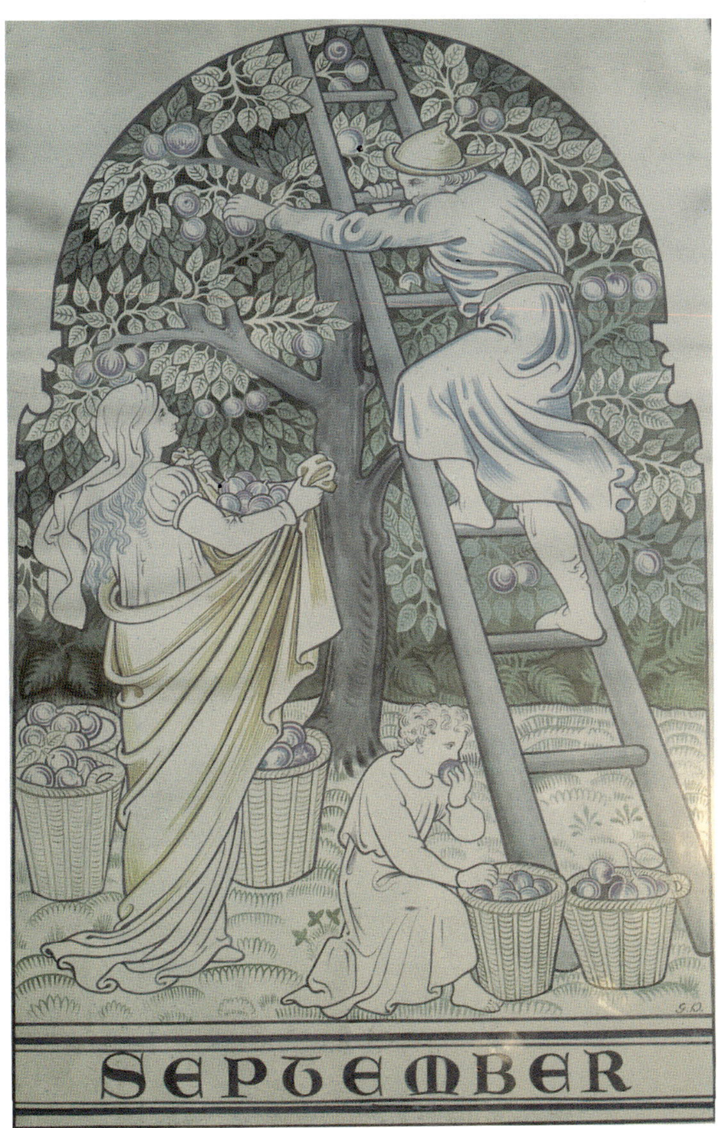

One of the original cartoons for the Labours of the Month now displayed in church tower.

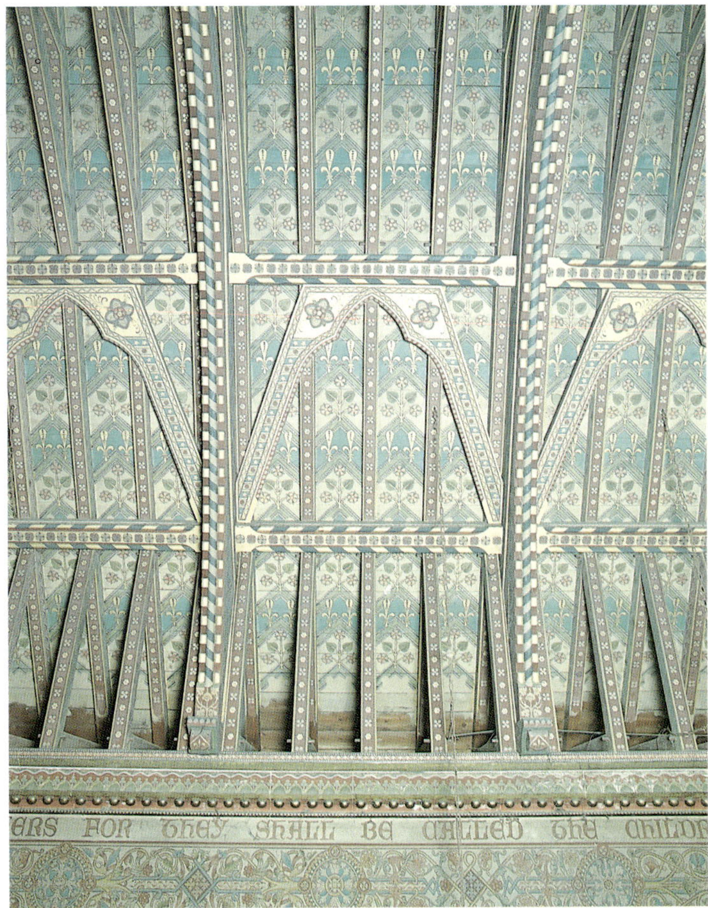

Chancel roof

worshipper moves physically from the Wisdom of the Old Testament to the Revelation of the New. The Genesis sequence beginning with the Creation and ending with the cursing of Cain is the first thing to meet one's eye on entering the church and the Creation story is supplemented and reinforced by the painting of Noah building his ark and collecting the animals on the wall above; the second stage, as it was then believed, in the establishment of the animal kingdom. This is balanced on the opposite wall by the Labours of the Months, a very old sequence originating in early mediaeval times, and usually illustrating the Signs of the Zodiac, which apart from hawking in May and the *vendage* in October show the usual monthly occupations of Sir Tatton's tenants and farm labourers. Scenes from the lives of Moses, Joseph and David complete the decoration of the nave. In the chancel the Annunciation, the Adoration and the Last Judgement represent the fundamental tenets of Christian belief, and on the chancel arch the Jesse Tree symbolising the descent of Christ from King David forms a connection between the Old and the New.

Two further points should be made before a detailed description of the paintings is attempted. First, the iconographical scheme at Garton is unparalleled in its scope. The only comparable series of paintings appears to be that designed for the ceiling of the nave of Ely Cathedral by H. S. Le Strange and T. Gambier Parry in 1858-65, where there is a sequence of Old and New Testament scenes set between saints and prophets and linked by images of King David and Jesse. Second, by some most fortunate chance, the twelve original cartoons for the Labours of the Months have survived, been framed, and hung in the tower. Cartoons on paper are naturally perishable, and subjected to rough treatment when in use; to find a whole set like this is most unusual.

The wall paintings at Garton were executed in the spirit fresco technique developed by Gambier Parry, which involves painting in a mixture of oil and resin-bound pigments on to primed plaster or stone, apart from the sequence of Labours of the Months where a different binding medium has been used giving these a yellowish tone. Over the years water penetration, dust and the smoke from oil lamps had caused decay and when the distinguished art historian Sir Nikolaus Pevsner compiled the *Yorkshire : York & The East Riding* volume of *The Buildings of England* in 1972 he wrote "It is essential that they be preserved". After his death in 1983 the Trustees of the Pevsner Memorial Trust decided, with the agreement of the parish, that the restoration of the paintings should be undertaken in his memory and the work was begun by Wolfgang Gärtner and Donald Smith in 1985 and completed in 1991. The accumulated dirt of over a hundred years has been cleaned away and damage caused by the damp repaired, returning the paintings to their original brilliance.

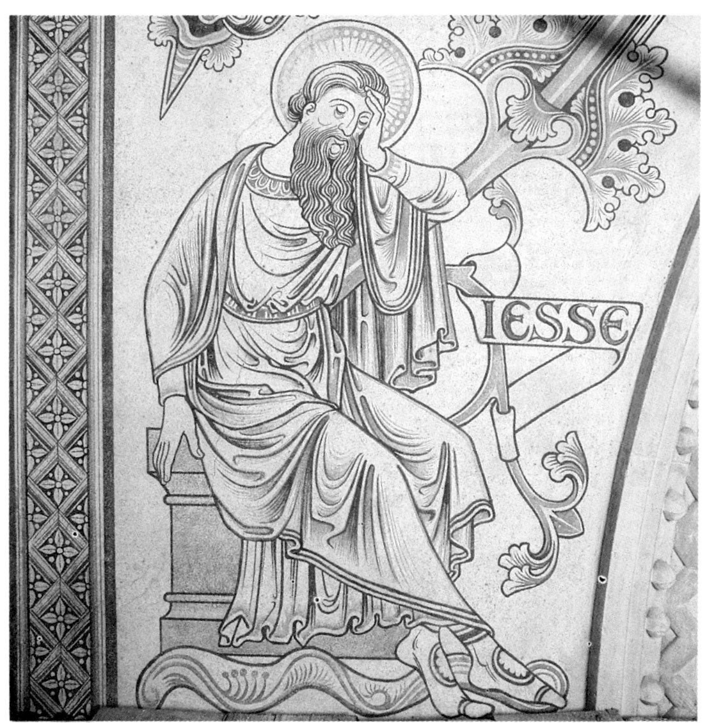

Nave – east wall, north side of Chancel arch.
Part of Jesse tree showing Jesse, father of King David.

NOTES ON THE WALL PAINTINGS AND THE STAINED GLASS, AND THEIR MEANING

THE NAVE — EAST WALL

Upper wall — above the triple opening the Virgin and Child enthroned, at the apex of the Jesse Tree. Insc: *Parvulus enim natus est nobis et filius natus est nobis,* and below, the Annunciation. Insc: *Ave Maria Grat. Plena*. The Jesse Tree is a symbolic representation of the ancestry of Christ and his descent from Jesse the father of King David as set out in the first chapter of St. Matthew's Gospel, but not every person included in the pedigree is shown here.

Lower wall — the Four Doctors of the Western Church. North side — St. Augustine of Hippo with his attribute, a heart. His two works the *Confessions* and the *City of God* are classics of sacred literature. St. Gregory the Great, elected Pope in 590, wears a triple papel tiara.
South side — St. Ambrose, Bishop of Milan, carries a scourge. St. Jerome, translator of the Bible into Latin (the Vulgate), wears cardinal's robes.

THE NAVE — NORTH WALL

Upper wall, on the west

In the roundel — the sacrifice of Abel. *He also brought of the firstlings of his flock and the fat thereof. And the LORD had respect unto Abel and to his offering.* Genesis 4.4.
Main panel — Insc: *Cain rose up against Abel*. Genesis 4.8. Abel's crook has been broken and the serpent, representing evil, appears.
West window splays — on the left Tubal Cain *an instructor of every artificer in brass and iron* with a hammer and lamp. Genesis 4.22. On the right Enoch *who was translated that he should not see death; and was not found, because God had translated him.* Hebrews 11.5. The stained glass shows Enoch being raised to heaven by six angels Insc: *Henoch non apar: quia tulit eum deus.*

Upper wall, centre west

In the roundel — the dove returning to Noah. *And the dove came to him in the evening; and, lo, in her mouth was an olive leaf pluckt off.* Genesis 8.11.
Main panel — Insc: *Thus did Noah according to all that God commanded him* - Noah with the Ark and the animals. Genesis 6.13-22.
Centre window splays — on the right, Isaac carrying the bundle of faggots, and on the left Abraham on his way to the land of Moriah to sacrifice his son, carrying a knife and the fire. The stained glass shows him about to sacrifice Isaac, the angel forbidding him and the ram caught in the thicket. Genesis 22.1-13. Insc: *Non extend: manum tuum super puerum.*

Upper wall, centre east

In the roundel — Isaac blessing his son Jacob who has disguised himself as the elder son Esau. His mother Rebekah watches, the dish of savoury meat is on the table. Genesis 27.18-29. *Thy brother came with subtilty, and hath taken away thy blessing.* Genesis 27.35.
Main panel — Insc: *I am Joseph your brother whom ye sold into Egypt* — Joseph identifying himself to his brothers. Genesis 45.4.

East window splays — on the left Moses with the Tables, on the right Aaron wearing his priestly garments and carrying a censer. Exodus 28.3-39. The stained glass shows Moses anointing Aaron. Leviticus 8.12. *And he poured the anointing oil upon Aaron's head and anointed him to sanctify him.* Insc: *Fundens sup cap Aaron unxit et m ft const.*

Upper wall, on the east

In the roundel — Moses and the burning bush. Exodus 3.1-6. *And the Angel of the Lord appeared unto him in a flame of fire out of the midst of a bush; and he looked and, behold, the bush burned with fire, and the bush was not consumed.*

Main panel — Insc: *He gave unto Moses two tables of stone* - Moses receiving the Tables of the Law on Mount Sinai, Joshua waits for him in the foreground. Exodus 24.12-13.

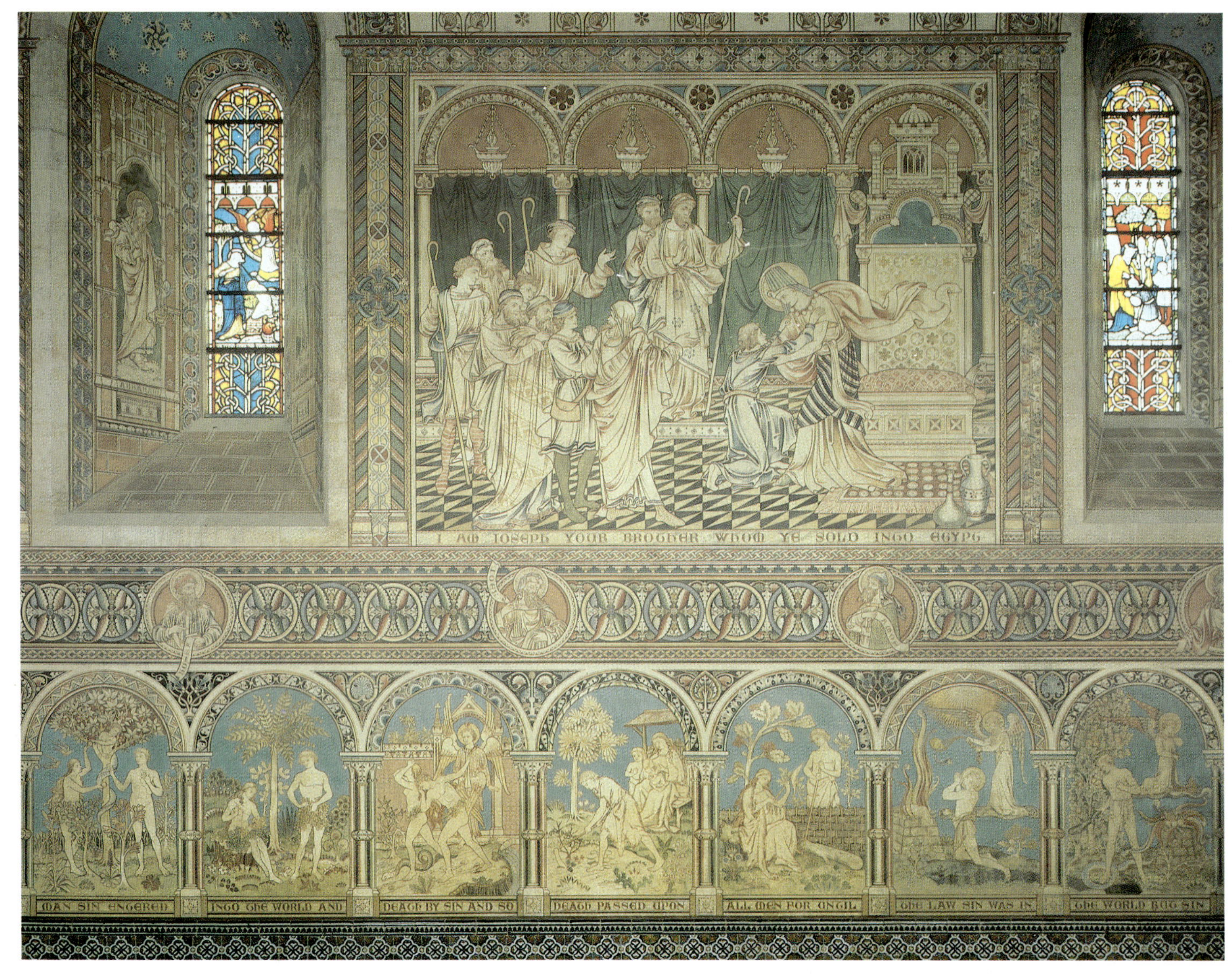

Nave – north wall. Joseph identifying himself to his brothers.
The arcade shows scenes of the Fall of Man.

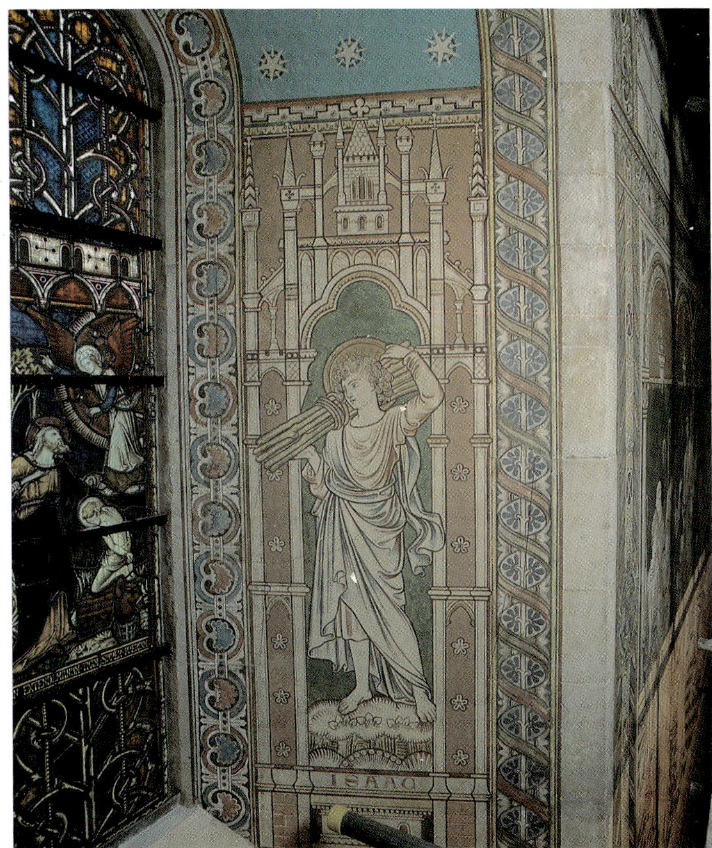

Left: Nave – north wall, centre window splay. Isaac carrying a bundle of faggots. The stained glass shows Isaac about to be sacrificed.

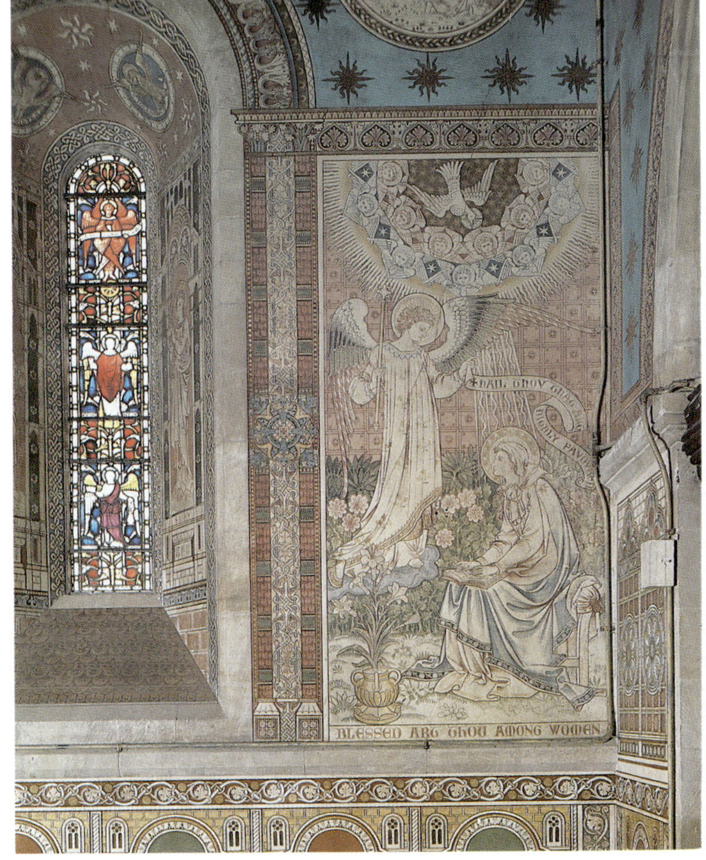

Right: Chancel – south wall. The Annunciation. The stained glass shows three of the Angelic Orders a seraph, a virtue and a dominion.

THE NAVE — NORTH WALL continued

Lower wall, below the windows — Roundels bearing heads of nine prophets, shown in the order in which their books appear in the Old Testament: Isaiah, Jeremiah, Ezekiel, Daniel, Hosea, Joel, Amos, Obadiah and Jonah.

Lower wall, in the arcade — the Genesis Creation myth and the Fall of Man. Insc: *Fear God and give glory to Him and worship him that made heaven and earth and the sea and the fountains of water. By one man sin entered into the world and death by sin and so death passed upon all men for until the law sin was in the world but sin is not imputed where there is no law.*
The scenes show, from west to east:

the spirit of God represented by a dove, moving upon the face of the waters, and the creation of light;

the creation of the firmament and the vision of the waters;

the creation of the sun, moon and stars;

the creation of vegetation;

the creation of the birds and fishes, including the whale;

the creation of Adam and the animals;

the creation of Eve;

Eve tempted by the serpent;

Adam and Eve after the Fall wearing aprons made of leaves;

Adam and Eve and the serpent expelled from the garden of Eden, the lush growth of the garden contrasted with thorns, thistles, cacti and weeds outside;

Adam digging and Eve with their sons Cain and Abel;

Eve spinning;

the sacrifice of Abel accepted by God;

the sacrifice of Cain rejected, the serpent lurks nearby;

Cain slays Abel;

Adam and Eve with Abel's body;

Cain and the serpent pursued by an avenging angel. Genesis 1-5.16.

Clayton and Bell used some of these designs again in stained glass made for the churches of Thixendale, built in 1868-70, and East Heslerton, completed in 1877, both new churches designed by Street for Sir Tatton.

THE NAVE — SOUTH WALL

West window splays — on the left Joshue with the sun which he commanded to stand still: *Sun stand thou still upon Gibeon; and thou Moon, in the valley of Ajalon. And the sun stood still, and the moon stayed, until the people had avenged themselves upon their enemies.* Joshua 10.12-13. On the right Hur, one of the elders of Israel, who with Aaron supported Moses during a crucial battle: *And Aaron and Hur stayed up his hands, the one on the one side, and the other on the other side; and his hands were steady until the going down of the sun. And Joshua discomfited Amalek and his people with the edge of the sword.* Exodus 17.12-13. The stained glass shows Samuel anointing David. Insc: *Samuel unxit eum in medio fratrum eius.* 1 Samuel 16.13.

Centre window splays — on the left Samuel holding a censer and on the right Samson with the jawbone of an ass and the column of the palace in Gaza. The stained glass shows the spies sent by Moses into the land of Canaan. Numbers 13.17-23. *And they came to the brook of Eshcol, and cut down from thence a branch with one cluster of grapes, and they bare it between two upon a staff.* Insc: *Portaverunt in vecte duo viri.*

On the east

Upper wall, in the roundel — Solomon building the Temple. 1 Kings 6.1. *In the fourth year of Solomon's reign over Israel, in the month Zif, which is the second month, ... he began to build the house of the Lord.*
Main panel — David the shepherd boy piping to his flock. 1 Samuel 17.15. *David went and returned from Saul to feed his father's sheep at Bethlehem.* Samuel had already anointed him the future king of Israel.

Centre east

Upper wall, in the roundel — an unidentified scene, a king prostrate outside a city and an angel bearing a shield and a sword.
Main panel — Insc: *This day will the Lord deliver thee into mine hand* —David confronts Goliath of Gath the champion of the Philistines, whom he killed with a sling shot. The serpent is at Goliath's feet. 1 Samuel 17.46.

Upper wall, centre west

In the roundels — two unidentified scenes, a dead king on a tomb mourned by a young man and two women, and a priest holding a spear, standing in front of two tents, between which a man lies asleep or dead.
Main panel — Insc: *Abner took him and brought him before Saul.* David brings the head of Goliath to Saul. 1 Samuel 17.57.

East window — the stained glass does not form part of the Old Testament sequence, but illustrates scenes from the Passion. Insc: at the top — *Propter quod et Jesus ut sanctificavit per suum sanguinem populum extra portam passus est* — the Crucifixion with Mary Salome and St. Mary Magdalene on the left, and the Virgin Mary and St. John to either side of the cross, on the right the centurion and other male bystanders; the sun in eclipse and the moon indicate that a great event is taking place. In the centre: Christ carrying the cross — Insc: *Languores nostras ipse tulit*; the Deposition — Insc: *Iri posuerunt Jesum*; Christ appearing to St. Mary Magdalene after the crucifixion — Insc: *Dicit ei Jesus noli me tangere*. At the bottom the Agony in the Garden, the Betrayal, Judas identifies Christ with a kiss and Christ crowned with thorns and mocked. Painted on the wall beneath the window are the arms of Sir Tatton Sykes on the left and of his wife, Cavendish-Bentinck quartered with Scott of Balcomie, on the right. They are dated 1874.

Lower wall, below the windows — Roundels bearing heads of the Old Testament prophets: Micah, Nahum, Habakkuk, Zephaniah, Haggai, and Zachariah.

Lower wall, in the arcade — the Labours of the Months. January — warming before fire, February — feasting, March — digging, April — sowing, May — hawking, June — gathering flowers, July — reaping, August —threshing, September — fruit picking, October — picking grapes, November — cutting firewood, December — pig killing.

Lunette above south door — St. Michael (patron saint of the church) and Insc: *This is the gate of the law and the righteous shall enter into it.* Psalm 118.20.

THE NAVE — WEST WALL

The Last Judgement: Insc: *Gather ye together first the tares and bind them in bundles to burn them but gather the wheat into my barn.* Matthew 13.30. — Christ in Majesty, adored and censed by angels, who on the left cut and bind sheaves of corn which they present to him, and on the right separate flowers from thorns, the flowers presented, the thorns thrown upon a fire. This is symbolic of the division of the elect from the damned in traditional representations of the Last Judgement.

Lower wall — the Four Doctors of the eastern Church.
North side — St. John Chrysostom, the Doctor of the Eucharist, Bishop of Constantinople and famous for his revision of the Greek liturgy. St. Athanasius, the champion of Orthodoxy against the Arians and patriarch of Alexandria.
South side — St. Gregory Nazianzen, the Divine, the theologian of Nazianzos in Cappadocia. St. Basil with the dove representing divine inspiration on his shoulder, Metropolitan of Caesarea who edited the Eucharistic Liturgy which bears his name.

West window in tower — St. John the Baptist with his staff and banner *Ecce Agnes Dei.* Insc: *St. Johannes Bap.* Below, the Baptism of Christ. Insc: *Hic est filius meus dilectus.* In the border seven doves inscribed with the names of virtues: *Sapientia Intellectus Consilium Fortitudo Scientia Pietas Timor.*

Under the tower are the original cartoons of The Labours of the Months.

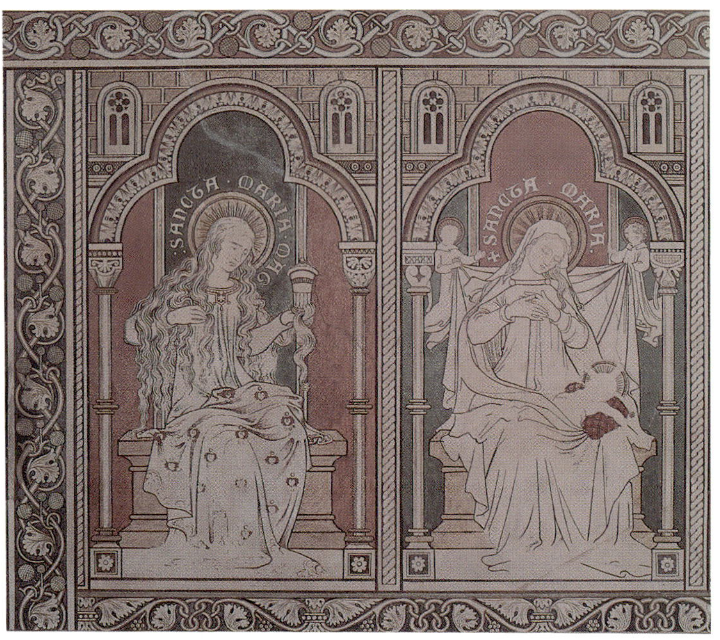

Above: Chancel – north wall. Saint Mary Magdalene and the Virgin Mary with the Infant Christ. The figure on the right shows the outline retouching technique used for badly decayed paintings.

To right at top: Chancel – north wall. Parable of the Good Samaritan.

To right at bottom: Chancel – south wall. Parable of wheat and tares.

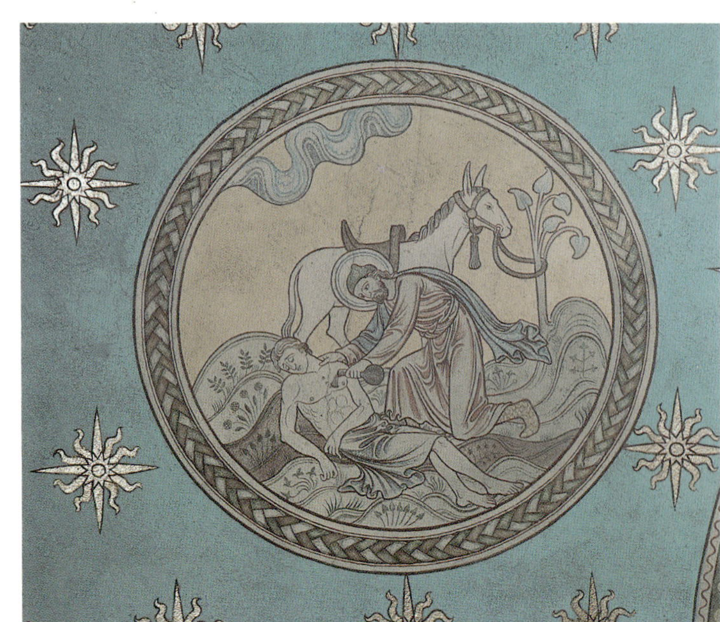

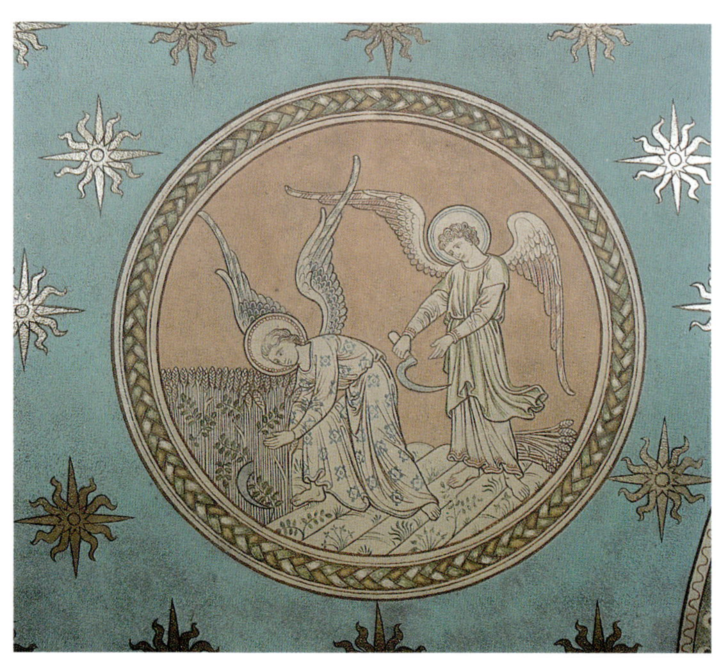

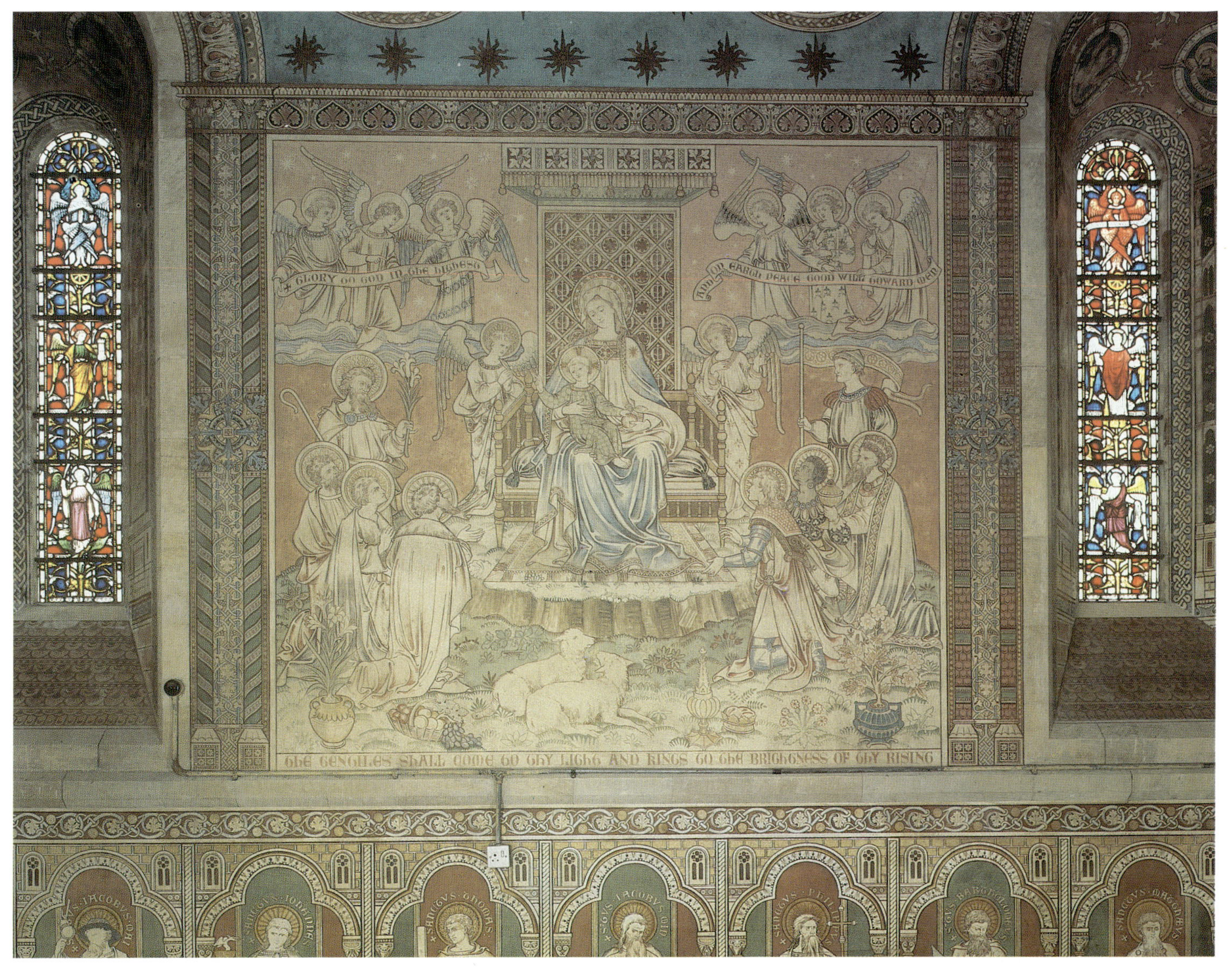

Chancel – south wall. Adoration scene with Virgin and Child enthroned in glory.

THE CHANCEL — EAST WALL

The east window splays are decorated with roundels containing busts of Old and New Testament figures and others connected with the early church in England. The central window has on the left the prophet Isaiah holding a scroll, and King David with his harp; on the right are St. Paul with his attribute of a sword and St. Peter. The left window has on the left Abraham holding the knife with which he intended to sacrifice his son Isaac, and Noah holding the ark and the sprig of olive which the dove brought when the flood abated; on the right are Joshua with the sun and a sword, and Moses holding the tables of the law. The right window has on the left St. Alban, the protomartyr of Britain, and St. Stephen, deacon and protomartyr who was stoned to death in Jerusalem, and so carries a stone; on the right the Venerable Bede whose *Ecclesiastical History of the English People* earned him the title of The Father of English History, and St. Augustine, the Apostle to the English. On either side of the windows are shown the Instruments of the Passion: a lantern, the purse containing the thirty pieces of silver, the chalice used at the Last Supper, the crown of thorns, the whip and scourge with which Christ was beaten, the ropes and the column to which he was tied, the spear and the sponge soaked in vinegar, the nails, the cross, the robe, the dice with which the soldiers gambled for Christ's garments, and the mocking label INRI, the initials of the Latin words of Jesus of Nazareth King of the Jews.

The reredos has a carved central panel of the Crucifixion with the Virgin Mary and St. John between kneeling angels. On the left is the Annunciation, the Archangel Gabriel appearing to the Virgin, and the Baptism of Christ in the river Jordan by St. John the Baptist. In both these panels the Holy Spirit appears in the form of a dove. On the right is the Entombment in which Christ's body is laid to rest by the Virgin, St. John, Mary Magdalene and Joseph of Arimathea, and the scene on the Road to Emmaus when Christ, unrecognised after his Resurrection, joined two of the disciples.

THE CHANCEL — SOUTH WALL

Three roundels — the Parable of the Wheat and the Tares. Matthew 13.24-30, 36-43. *The Kingdom of heaven is likened unto a man which sowed good seed in his field: But while men slept his enemy came and sowed tares among the wheat...* When this was discovered he said *Let both grow together until the harvest; and in the time of harvest I will say to the reapers, gather ye together first the tares, and bind them in bundles to burn them; but gather the wheat into my barn.* Jesus explained: *He that soweth the good seed is the son of man; the field is the world; the good seed are the children of the kingdom; but the tares are the children of the wicked one; the enemy that sowed them is the devil; the harvest is the end of the world; and the reapers are the angels.*

Main panel — Insc: The Gentiles shall come to thy light and Kings to the brightness of thy rising. Isaiah 60.3. —The Virgin Mary and the infant Christ enthroned and adored by angels, some of whom carry scrolls reading *Glory to God in the Highest* and *And on earth peace good will towards men.* The shepherds on the left accompanied by sheep, the three Magi on the right offer their gifts of gold, frankincense and myrrh. The traditional setting of this scene is the stable at Bethlehem, but here the Virgin and child in glory has been combined with the usual elements of the Adoration. The three Magi are traditionally shown as young, middle aged and old, and there is a similar tradition that one of them was black.

West panel — Insc: *Blessed art thou among women.* Luke 1.28. The Annunciation — the Archangel Gabriel carrying his wand of office as the messenger of God and in his left hand a scroll inscribed with his greeting to the Virgin Mary, when he tells her that she is to be the mother of Christ. She is holding a book, an allusion to the belief that the Archangel interrupted her reading at Isaiah 7.14: *Behold, a virgin shall conceive, and bear a son and shall call his name Immanuel.* The pot of lilies is an almost invariable accompaniment to this scene, lilies being an emblem of the Virgin signifying purity. The Holy Spirit descends in the form of a dove.

East window splays — the Evangelists St. Matthew and St. Mark with their symbols, an angel and a lion, in roundels above.

West window splays — the Evangelists St. Luke and St. John with their symbols, a bull and an eagle, in roundels above.

Lower wall — the Apostles seated beneath an arcade:

Sanctus Petrus — St. Peter with his attribute, the keys, a reference to Christ's words *I will give unto thee the keys of the kingdom of heaven.* Matthew 16.19.

Sanctus Andreas — St. Andrew, the brother of St. Peter, with the saltire cross on which he was crucified at Patras in Achaia.

Sanctus Jacobus Maj. — St. James the Great, the son of Zebedee and Salome, the first of the apostles to be martyred under Herod Agrippa. He is the patron saint of pilgrims and has a palmer's hat and staff. The boat is that in which his disciples set sail with his body, and which with no sail or rudder bore them to Santiago de Compostella in Spain, where the saint's relics became an object of pilgrimage.

Sanctus Johannes — St. John the Evangelist also known as St. John the Divine, brother of St. James the Great, holding his attibute, a chalice from which a snake or a dragon is emerging. A priest of Diana challenged him to drink a cup of poison which he rendered harmless by making the sign of the cross over it.

Sanctus Thomas — St. Thomas holding a set square. In the 3rd century *Acts of Thomas* the saint is said to have been taken to India to work as a carpenter for King Gundaphorus, but spent his time preaching and teaching, causing such a disturbance that he was put to death by being run through with spears.

Sanctus Jacobus Min. — St. James the Less, with a club, a cousin of Our Lord and first bishop of Jerusalem. Martyred there by being thrown from the Temple and beaten to death.

Sanctus Philippus — St. Philip with a cross staff. He preached in Asia Minor and martyred at Hierapolis in Phrygia.

Sanctus Bartholomeus — St. Bartholomew holding a knife. He was martyred by being flayed alive, after preaching in Asia Minor, north-west India and Greater Armenia.

Sanctus Matthæus — St. Matthew the Evangelist with a money box. He was a tax collector in Capernaum before being called to be one of Jesus' disciples.

Sanctus Judas — St. Jude Thaddaeus with a boat. He was the brother of St. James the Less and a son of Mary the wife of Cleophas, and went with Simon to Edessa and Mesopotamia where they caused idols to be overthrown, and were both killed by pagan priests. The boat is a symbol of his travels.

Sanctus Simon — St. Simon the Zealot, brother of Jude, preached in Egypt and Persia and martyred there. He was a fisherman and his usual symbol is a fish; here he carries a saw, which may be the instrument of his martyrdom.

Sanctus Matthias — St. Matthias, chosen by the other apostles to take the place of Judas Iscariot, holding a halberd. He was martyred in Jerusalem by being stoned and then beheaded.

THE CHANCEL — NORTH WALL

Three roundels — the Parables of the mustard seed, the Prodigal Son and the Good Samaritan. *The Kingdom of heaven is like to a grain of mustard seed, which a man took and sowed in his field; which is indeed the least of all seeds; but when it is grown, it is the greatest among herbs, and becometh a tree, so that the birds of the air come and lodge in the branches thereof.* Matthew 13.31-32. The return of the Prodigal Son. *But when he was yet a great way off, his father saw him, and had compassion, and ran, and fell upon his neck, and kissed him.* Luke 15.20. The man who fell among thieves was ignored by other travellers *But a certain Samaritan, as he journeyed, came where he was; and when he* *saw him, he had compassion on him. And he went to him, and bound up his wounds, pouring in oil and wine, and set him on his own beast. Luke 10.33-34.*

Main panel — The Last Judgement — Insc: *He shall come again with glory to judge both the quick and the dead whose kingdom shall have no end.* The Last Judgement shows Christ enthroned, beneath him the Archangel Michael with the sword and scales of justice in which the good and the bad are weighed. On the left St. Peter with his attribute of the keys of the Kingdom of Heaven entrusted to him after his confession of faith, five of the disciples and the prophets Micah, Hosea, Jeremiah, Malachi and Ezekiel. On the right St. John the Baptist, six disciples and the prophets Amos, Obadiah, Daniel, Jonah and two others. Below, angels sound the last trump and the dead arise, the blessed, who include children and a bishop, assisted by angels, and the damned driven by angels with flaming swords into the mouth of hell. Among the latter is a miser clutching his money bag.

Window splays — On the left, St. John the Baptist with the Agnus Dei in a roundel above, and on the right the Virgin Mary with the dove of the Holy Spirit in the roundel.

Below — female saints and holy women seated beneath an arcade. From west to east:
Sancta Elizabetha — St. Elizabeth the mother of St. John the Baptist with her son and his attribute, a lamb.
Maria Bethania — Mary of Bethany, the sister of Lazarus, reading a book and representing the contemplative way of life.
Martha Bethania — Martha of Bethany her sister, holding a tray with a flagon, representing the active way of life. When the sisters entertained Christ, Mary sat at Jesus' feet, causing Martha, who was preparing the meal, to complain that she *was cumbered about much serving*. Luke 10.40.
Eunice — the mother of Timothy, probably converted by St. Paul on his first visit to Lystra.
Sancta Maria Mag — St. Mary Magdalene, the woman who was a sinner, with the pot of ointment with which she anointed the feet of Christ, drying them with her hair.
Sancta Maria — the Virgin Mary with the infant Christ.
Sancta Salome — holding a jar of spices. Mary Salome was one of the women present at the Crucifixion; she bore spices to the sepulchre to anoint Christ's body.

Aumbry — a recess for vessels for communion, decorated with wheat ears, vine leaves and grapes representing the bread and wine of the communion.

To the right — Dorcas — Tabitha of Joppa, a woman *full of good works* raised from the dead by St. Peter. Acts 9.40.

THE CHANCEL — WEST WALL

Above the triple opening — Roundel with Agnus Dei.

Over the Chancel Arch — Two roundels. That on the left illustrates the Parable of the Talents.*A man travelling into a far country, who called his own servants and delivered unto them his goods. And unto one he gave five talents, to another two, and to another one.* Matthew 25.14-15. On the right the Parable of the Unmerciful Servant. *His lord, after he called him, said unto him, O thou wicked servant, I forgave thee all that debt, because thou desirest me; shouldest not thou also have had compassion on thy fellow-servants, even as I had pity on thee? And his lord was wroth, and delivered him to the tormentors.* Matthew 18.32-34.

Below. To left Sanctus Paulus — St. Paul the evangelist to the Gentiles holding both a sword, the symbol of his martyrdom by beheading in Rome, and his epistles.

To right Sancta Anna — St. Anne with the young Virgin Mary.

The painters who worked on the chancel signed their names on the roof. They were J. Smith, A. Thomas, and John Cadman of London and James Black, who dated their signatures June 1873.

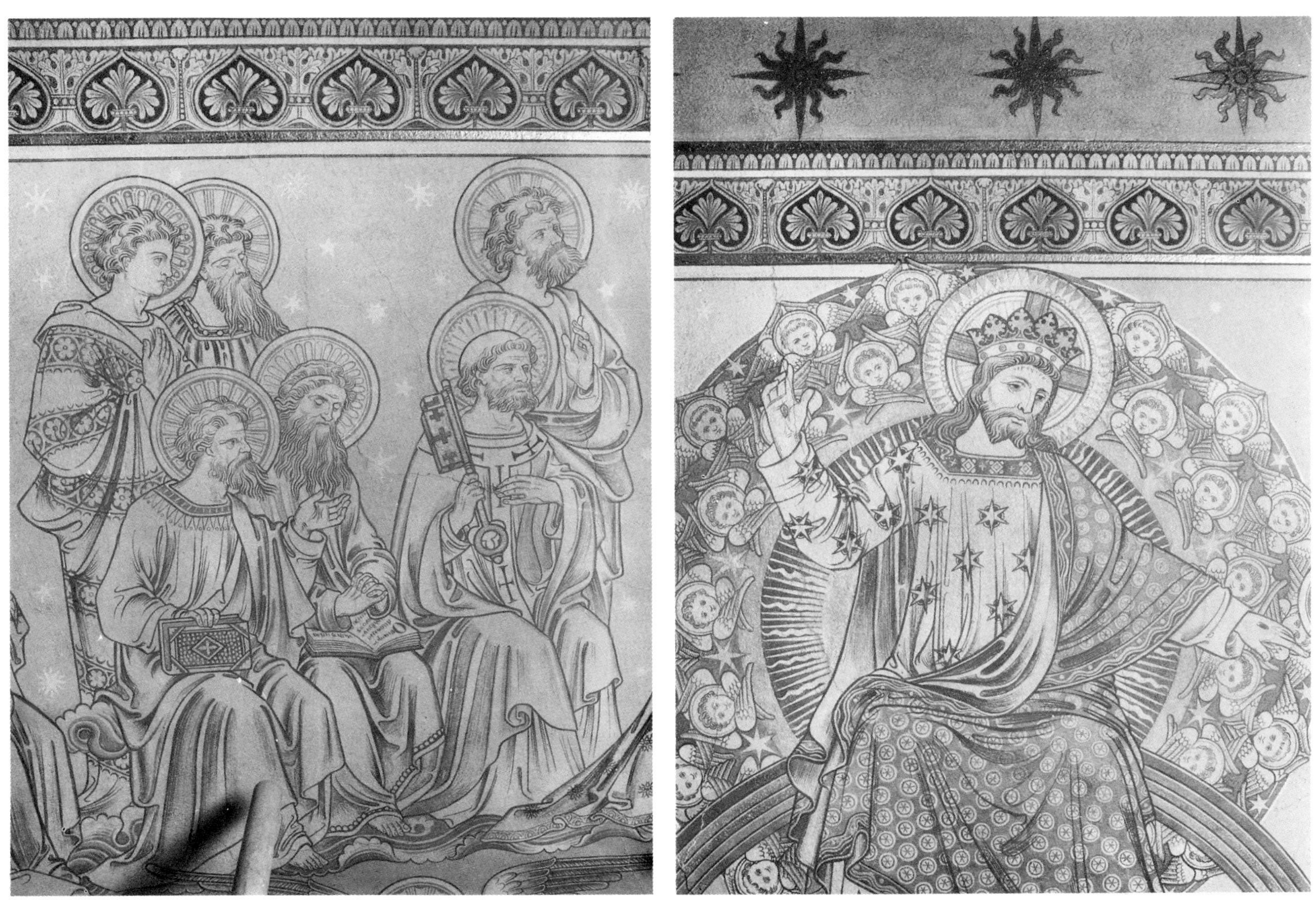

Chancel – north wall. Two scenes from the Last Judgement. On the right Christ enthroned. On the left St. Peter with the key and five of the disciples.

THE CHANCEL — STAINED GLASS

The stained glass in the chancel depicts the nine orders of angels described in mediaeval angelology and enumerated first in the Pseudo-Dionysius. These are divided into three hierarchies each of three orders which consist of seraphim, cherubim, thrones, dominations, principalities, powers, virtues, archangels and angels.

The window in the east gable has glass showing Christ enthroned in glory with a cruciform nimbus raising his right hand in blessing, thus displaying the wound caused by a nail at his crucifixion. In his left hand he holds a book inscribed with the letters Alpha and Omega, the first and last letters of the Greek alphabet, long used as a sign of the omnipotence of God. *I am Alpha and Omega, the beginning and the ending, saith the Lord, which is, and which was, and which is to come, the Almighty.* Revelation 1.8. Insc: *Tu Rex Gloriae.* Beneath are the emblems of the four Evangelists: St. Matthew, a winged man, St. John, an eagle, St. Mark, a winged lion, and St. Luke, a winged ox. These figures are described in both the Old and New Testaments: *As for the likeness of their faces, they four had the face of a man, and the face of a lion, on the right side; and they four had the face of an ox on the left side; they four also had the face of an eagle.* Ezekiel 1.10. *Round about the throne, were four beasts full of eyes before and behind. And the first beast was like a lion, and the second beast like a calf, and the third beast had a face as a man, and the fourth beast was like a flying eagle.* Revelation 4.6-7.

The three windows below have glass with censing angels and music-making angels playing a viol, harp, trumpet, cymbals, triangle, organ, lute, oboe, cello, flute and drum. Half length angels above carry scrolls inscribed *Alleluia, Alleluia.*

In the south east window there are figures representing a cherub, a throne carrying a crenellated tower and a principality, who has a sceptre.

In the south west window others represent a seraph, a virtue, bearing a chalice and an orb, and a dominion with a crown and a censer.

The north window has the archangel St. Michael, the patron saint of Garton church, with the sword and scales, an angel bearing the souls of the blessed to paradise, and a power bearing symbols of chastisement, a birch and chain.

The writer wishes to acknowledge help received from G. K. Beaulah, David Findlay, Paul Joyce, Susan Neave, John Newman and Anthony Quiney.

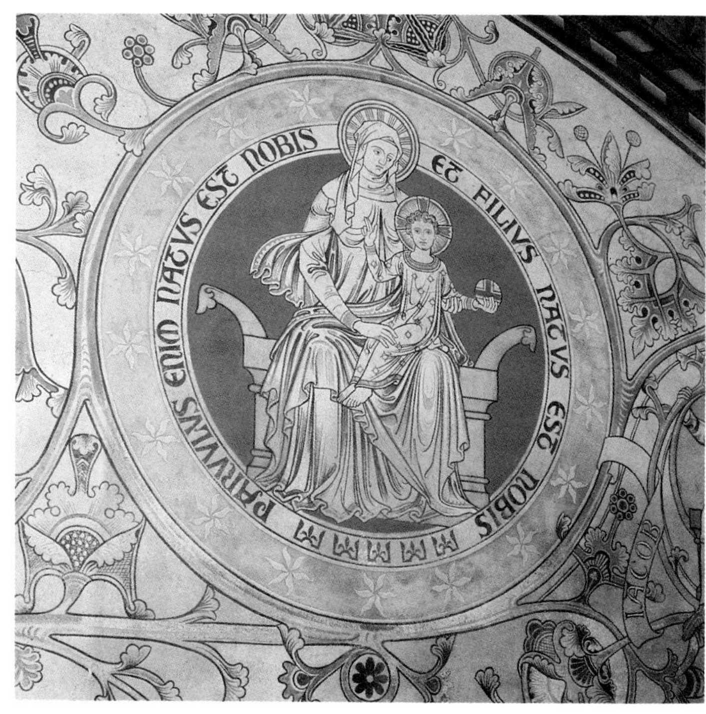

Nave – east wall. Virgin and Child at the top of the tree of Jesse.

Nave – north wall. Creation scenes in arcade.

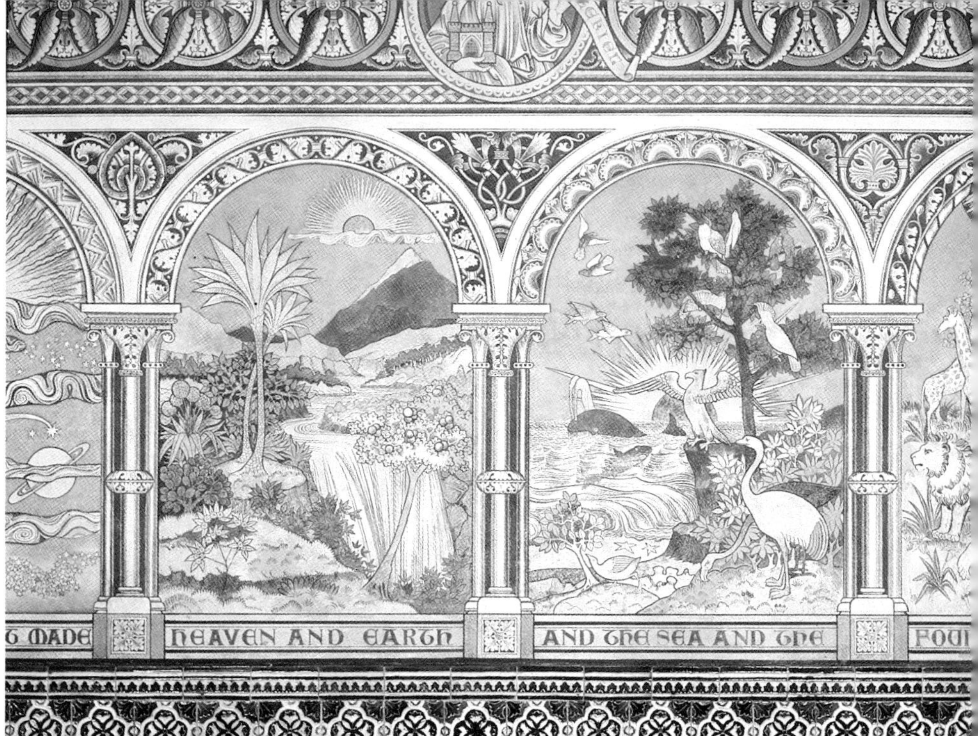

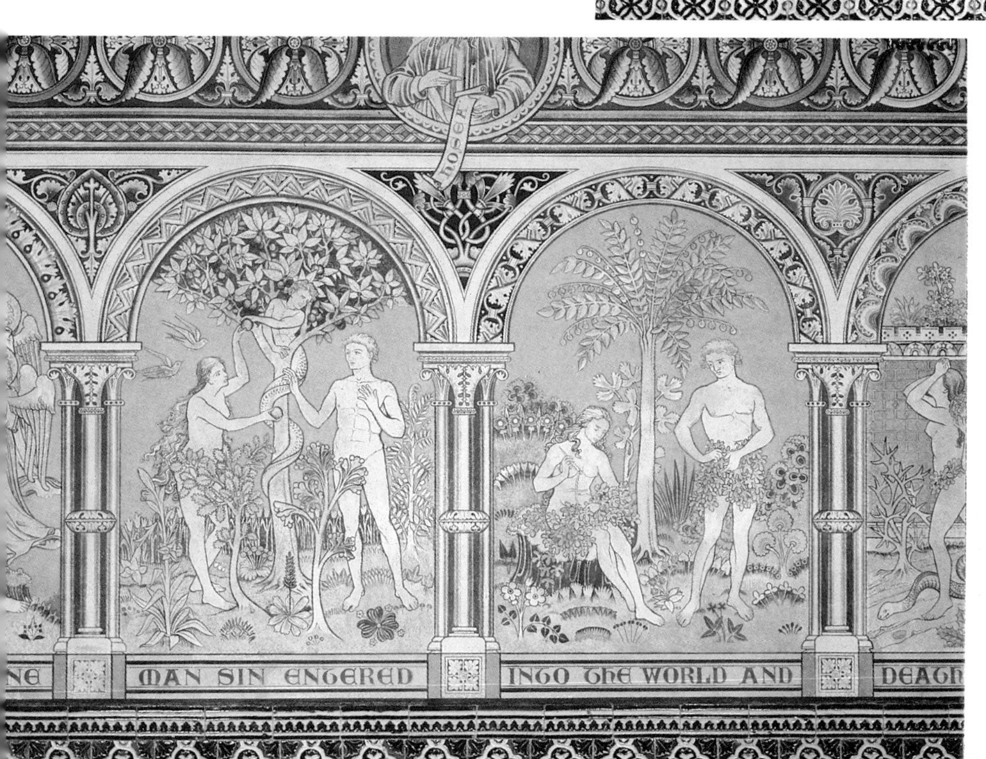

Nave – north wall. Scenes of the Fall of Man in arcade.

CONSERVATION OF THE WALLPAINTINGS

The wallpaintings at Garton-on-the-Wolds were executed by Clayton & Bell in the 'spirit fresco' technique, devised by Thomas Gambier Parry (1816-88). This involved the use of a mixture of oil and resin-bound pigments on primed plaster.

In the period of over a century since the paintings were executed they had become very dirty from engrained dust and smoke. But, far more damagingly, they had been affected by damp, resulting in salt efflorescence over much of their surface and, in a number of areas, the total breakdown of the oil and resin medium, leaving the pigment friable and unstable. Fortunately, the plaster support remained in good condition almost everywhere except on the south wall of the nave, where over an area of up to two square metres the plaster had detached itself from the wall and was about to break away.

The conservators, Donald Smith and Wolfgang Gärtner, after a trial season in 1986, worked for five full seasons, 1987-91, cleaning, consolidating where necessary and repainting the limited areas where the original painted surface had been lost. Each season lasted for about five weeks in midsummer, and the conservators, with the help of one or two assistants, were able to cover no more than one square metre per day. The sequence of conservation work was (1) removal of surface salt efflorescences, (2) consolidation of hollow sounding plaster and of flaking or powdery paint, (3) surface cleaning, (4) small repairs to plaster losses, (5) reconstruction of missing decoration/forms and other retouching. Lost decorative backgrounds (as, for example, at the top of the east wall of the chancel) were totally repainted in a replica of the original; but figure work was only 'reintegrated', so that it is apparent on close inspection that the painting is new work, while from a distance the overall design looks complete.

Several areas posed special problems. An attempt had been made in the past to restore parts of the paintings on the west wall of the nave, producing a different tonality. The figures of the four doctors of the Church on the nave east wall had been totally repainted about twenty years ago. The overpainting here had to be removed and the very damaged original figures reintegrated. The detached plaster on the nave south wall had to be cut away and reattached. Most of the painted surface could be saved, but a small area along its lower edge was recreated. The scenes of the Labours of the Months, in the bottom register on this wall, were painted almost directly on to prepared stonework. This saved them from disintegration, but it is the reason why these scenes differ tonally from the rest of the wallpaintings.

The problem of salt efflorescence is also particularly troublesome here: salts are showing signs of recurrence already. The Trust and the parish are collaborating in a scheme to monitor the environment of the church interior, with a view to providing in due course more stable conditions for the wallpaintings.